Hammer
The Hyperactive Hound

Hammer
The Hyperactive Hound

By Rachel Davis

Illustrated by Morgan Spicer

To my students, for teaching me more than I could have ever taught them.

"Bye Mom, I love you," Hammer said as he reached over to hug her.

"I love you more, Hammer. Have a great first day. Make sure to take your time with your work and ask for breaks when you need them."

"I know, Mom, I know," Hammer said as he grabbed his backpack and lunchbox and jumped out of the car.

Hammer was so excited for his first day of school that he didn't see the branch lying in front of him as he ran toward the schoolhouse. *Thump!*

"Awwww man," Hammer mumbled. He picked up the salami and cheese sandwich that fell out of his lunchbox and threw it in a nearby garbage pail.

Mrs. Barkley, the hall monitor, greeted Hammer as he walked into the building.

"Hello, I'm Mrs. Barkley. Can I help you find your classroom?"

"Yes please! I'm Hammer and I'm new here!" Hammer said.

Mrs. Barkley smiled, winked, and pointed to the blue door across the hall.

"Thanks and have a great day!" Hammer turned toward the door. He was so excited about starting his first day and making new friends!

Hammer walked up to the door of his new classroom. Before he could open it, the door swung open, and friendly Mrs. York stuck her paw out to greet him.

"You must be Hammer!" she declared. "You are the last one here, so please walk in quietly and take a seat in the third row, behind Sabrina."

"Ok," Hammer said eagerly.

Mrs. York's classroom was a joyful place.
Hammer couldn't stop looking all around the
room at the colorful decorations on the walls.
There was a reading corner in the back,
and even a turtle named Marley!

Hammer started down the aisle toward his seat. He was so enchanted by everything in the room, that he bumped into everyone.

"Ouch! Awe! Hey watch it!" chimed Sandy, Lola, and Zeus.

"I'm sorry guys, I'm really sorry," Hammer said nervously to his new classmates.

"Attention everyone, this is Hammer. Hammer is new to Howard Wesley Elementary and I am hoping that you will all make him feel welcome. Now, I am going to need someone to buddy up with Hammer and show him around today!"

"Hmmmmmm, Bremen? Would you like to help out?" Mrs. York asked, a bit forcefully.

Bremen glanced up from sketching on his binder.
"Yeah sure, I'll do it Mrs. York," he said.

Then he put his head back down and continued with his drawings.
Hammer couldn't wait to hang out with his new buddy.

"Alrighty pups, let's get started. Please take out a pencil and we'll begin a simple getting to know you exercise," began Mrs. York.

Before Mrs. York could say anything else,
Hammer's paw shot up in the air.

"I don't have a pencil!"
he yelled out.

Mrs. York was a little shocked.

"Alright Hammer, next time, please wait for me to call on you. Does anyone have a pencil to lend to Hammer?"

"I do," Sabrina said.

"I promise to give it back," Hammer told her.

As Mrs. York started her lesson, Hammer started tapping the pencil on his desk loudly.

"SHHHHH! Geez, what's up with this pup?" Lola whispered to Sandy. "Yeah, he's really annoying and loud," Sandy said.

Hammer heard every word. He dropped his head as a tear rolled down his cheek.

"Why does this always happen to me?" he thought.

He looked out the window at the basketball court.

"I wish I could show the pups in my class my basketball skills, then they'd think I'm cool," he thought, and his mind started to wander.

An hour later, the bell rang. Hammer looked up with surprise. He couldn't believe the class was already over!

"Wow I must have been daydreaming," he thought. He hopped out of his seat with his lunch box in one paw and basketball in the other.

Hammer walked into the cafeteria, and saw that the only seat left was next to Bremen, the super cool pup from class, who was supposed to show him around.

Hammer dashed over and plopped down next to him.

"Hey buddy, what's up?" Hammer smiled.

"Hey Hammer," Bremen said. "It's cool that you sit here today but my best friend, Bentley, will be back tomorrow and that's his seat, ok?"

"No problem, want to shoot some hoops after lunch?" Hammer asked, with his mouth full of food and mustard on his chin.

"Sure Hammer, let's see if you are any good, dude," Bremen grinned.

As they passed the girls' table, Lola whispered to Sandy, "That pup thinks he is going to be a good basketball player."

"Yeah right," Sandy replied. "Bremen will totally show him up. He is way too hyper."

"I bet he can't even follow the rules. We have to see this." Lola grabbed Sandy's paw and they ran outside to watch.

When the girls got to the basketball court, they couldn't believe their eyes! There was Hammer, weaving in and out of Bremen's legs and dribbling as fast as lighting!

He scored a layup and a stunned Bremen gave him a high-five.

"Dude, where did you learn how to play like that?" Bremen asked.

"I practice all of the time. I dribble in my house, I dribble in my driveway, I even dribble when I eat breakfast," Hammer said eagerly.

"It's my favorite thing to do. Sometimes I have trouble concentrating in school, and people laugh at me because I'm clumsy, but when I play basketball it's all I care about," Hammer gleamed.

"Hammer, you rock! Your dribbling skills are super cool…do you think you could teach me some moves?" Bremen asked.

"Totally!" Hammer's smile stretched from ear to ear.

That day after school, the pups practiced until the sun went down. From then on, Hammer helped Bremen with his dribbling, and Bremen sat next to Hammer in class to help him stay organized and remind him to raise his hand before speaking.

Both pups learned something from each other, and they became best buds.

Word traveled quickly around Howard Wesley Elementary of Hammer's basketball skills.

Soon, during every recess the bleachers were packed with students coming to see

HAMMER THE HYPERACTIVE HOUND!

Made in the USA
San Bernardino, CA
08 December 2016